101 Homestyle FAVORITES

Gooseberry Patch
2500 Farmers Dr., #110
Columbus, OH 43235

www.gooseberrypatch.com
1·800·854·6673

Copyright 2008, Gooseberry Patch 978-1-933494-19-7
Ninth Printing, March, 2012

Gooseberry Patch *cookbooks*

Since 1992, we've been publishing our own country cookbooks for every kitchen and for every meal of the day! Each title has hundreds of budget-friendly recipes, using ingredients you already have on hand in your pantry.

In addition, you'll find helpful tips and ideas on every page, along with our hand-drawn artwork and plenty of personality. Their lay-flat binding makes them so easy to use...they're sure to become a fast favorite in your kitchen.

Call us toll-free at
1•800•854•6673
and we'd be delighted to tell you all about our newest titles!

Shop with us online anytime at
www.gooseberrypatch.com

Send us your favorite recipe!

*and the memory that makes it special for you!** If we select your recipe for a brand-new **Gooseberry Patch** cookbook, your name will appear right along with it...and you'll receive a FREE copy of the book!

Submit your recipe on our website at
www.gooseberrypatch.com

Or mail to:

Gooseberry Patch • Attn: Cookbook Dept.
2500 Farmers Dr., #110 • Columbus, OH 43235

*Please include the number of servings and all other necessary information!

Have a taste for more?

Visit **www.gooseberrypatch.com** to join our **Circle of Friends**!

- Free recipes, tips and ideas plus a complete cookbook index
- Get special email offers and our monthly E-letter delivered to your inbox
- Find local stores with **Gooseberry Patch** cookbooks, calendars and organizers

CONTENTS

Dedication

To everyone who loves a good meal with
family & friends as much as we do!

Appreciation

A hearty thanks to all of you who opened
your hearts and your recipe boxes!

Pepperoni Puffs

1 c. all-purpose flour
1 t. baking powder
1 c. milk
1 egg, beaten
1 c. shredded Cheddar cheese
1-1/2 c. pepperoni, diced

Combine flour, baking powder, milk, egg and cheese; mix well. Stir in pepperoni; let stand for 15 minutes. Spoon into greased mini muffin cups, filling 3/4 full. Bake at 350 degrees for 25 to 35 minutes, until golden. Makes 2 dozen.

7

Marcia Marcoux
Charlton, MA
Serve with warmed pizza sauce for dipping.

Always-Requested Spinach Dip

1 c. mayonnaise
2 c. sour cream
1.8-oz. pkg. leek soup mix
4-oz. can water chestnuts,
    drained and chopped
10-oz. pkg. frozen chopped
    spinach, thawed and drained
1 round loaf pumpernickel bread

Combine mayonnaise, sour cream,
soup mix, water chestnuts and spinach;
mix well. Chill overnight. Slice off
top of loaf; gently tear out center,
reserving bread for dipping. Spoon
dip into center of loaf. Serve chilled,
surrounded with reserved bread pieces
for dipping. Serves 8.

Jennifer Kann
Dayton, OH

Is there anyone who
doesn't love this
tasty dip?

Touchdown Pinwheels

2 8-oz. pkgs. cream cheese,
   softened
1-oz. pkg. ranch salad dressing
   mix
2 green onions, chopped
5 12-inch flour tortillas
3/4 c. green olives with
   pimentos, chopped
3/4 c. black olives, chopped
4-1/2 oz. can chopped green
   chiles, drained
4-oz. jar chopped pimentos,
   drained

9

Combine cream cheese, dressing
mix and onions. Blend well; spread
evenly over one side of each tortilla.
Stir together olives, chiles and
pimentos; spoon over cream cheese
mixture. Roll up each tortilla
jelly-roll style; wrap each in plastic
wrap. Chill for at least 2 hours;
cut into one-inch slices. Makes
about 4 dozen.

Roberta Steele
Rock Hall, MD

Tote 'em to a party...
place the rolled tortillas
in a cooler and slice
them after you arrive.

Robert's Corn Dip

3 11-oz. cans sweet corn &
   diced peppers, drained
7-oz. can chopped green chiles
6-oz. can chopped jalapeños,
   drained and liquid added
   to taste
1/2 c. green onion, chopped
1 c. mayonnaise
1 c. sour cream
1 t. pepper
1/2 t. garlic powder
16-oz. pkg. shredded sharp
   Cheddar cheese
corn chips

Mix all ingredients except corn chips
together and refrigerate. Serve with
corn chips for scooping. Makes about
6 cups.

Carole Snodgrass
Rolla, MO

This dip is sooo delicious!
The flavor is even better
if it's made 2 days
ahead of time.

Zesty Black Bean Salsa

15-1/2 oz. can black beans,
 drained and rinsed
15-1/4 oz. can corn, drained
3/4 c. red pepper, diced
1/2 c. green onion, sliced
1/3 c. fresh cilantro, chopped
1/4 c. lime juice
1 t. ground cumin
1/4 t. garlic salt
tortilla chips

Combine beans, corn, pepper,
onion and cilantro; mix well. In a
separate bowl, whisk together lime
juice, cumin and garlic salt; pour
over bean mixture and toss gently.
Serve with tortilla chips. Makes
4 cups.

Beverly Ray
Brandon, FL

Spoon over grilled
chicken or fish for
a fresh new taste.

11

7-Layer Mexican Dip

16-oz. can refried beans
2 c. sour cream
1-1/4 oz. pkg. taco seasoning mix
2 avocados, pitted, peeled and
   mashed
2 t. lemon juice
3 cloves garlic, minced
2 c. shredded Cheddar cheese
4 green onions, diced
1/4 c. black olives, sliced
1 tomato, diced
tortilla chips

Spread beans in the bottom of a
10" round or square clear glass dish;
set aside. Combine sour cream and
seasoning mix; spread over beans. Mix
avocados, lemon juice and garlic; layer
over sour cream mixture. Sprinkle
with cheese; top with onions, olives
and tomato. Serve with tortilla chips.
Serves 8.

Renee Purdy
Mount Vernon, OH
Cut corn tortillas into
wedges and bake at
350 degrees for 5 minutes,
until crisp. Add salt to
taste...terrific!

Homemade Guacamole

3 avocados, pitted, peeled
  and mashed
1/2 c. tomato, chopped
1/4 c. onion, chopped
2 t. garlic, minced
1 T. fresh cilantro, chopped
1 t. salt
1 t. pepper
1 t. cayenne pepper
1 t. chili powder
1/2 t. hot pepper sauce
tortilla chips

Combine ingredients except
tortilla chips in order listed. Mix
well; chill. Serve with tortilla chips.
Makes about 2 cups.

13

Kim Secord
Hopewell Junction, NY
A ripe avocado will
yield when squeezed
gently in the palm
of the hand.

Hot Caramel Apple Cider

1/2 gal. apple cider
1/2 c. brown sugar, packed
1-1/2 t. cider vinegar
1 t. vanilla extract
4-inch cinnamon stick
6 whole cloves
1 orange, sliced
Optional: 1/2 c. apple jack liqueur
Garnish: 1/3 c. caramel ice cream
   topping

Combine all ingredients except topping in a slow cooker. Cover; cook on low setting for 5 to 6 hours. Strain; discard spices and orange. Serve in mugs, drizzling a teaspoonful of topping into each mug. Serves 16.

Kimberly Hancock
Murrieta, CA

Fill a slow cooker before going out for a fall hayride...the spicy aroma will fill the house!

Jo Ann's Holiday Brie

13.2-oz. pkg. Brie cheese
1/4 c. caramel ice cream topping
1/2 c. sweetened dried
    cranberries
1/2 c. dried apricots, chopped
1/2 c. chopped pecans
1 loaf crusty French bread, sliced,
    toasted and buttered

Place cheese on an ungreased
microwave-safe serving plate;
microwave on high setting for
10 to 15 seconds. Cut out a wedge
to see if center is soft. If center
is still firm, return to microwave
for another 5 to 10 seconds, until
cheese is soft and spreadable. Watch
carefully, as center will begin to melt
quickly. Drizzle with caramel topping;
sprinkle with fruit and nuts. Serve
with toasted slices of crusty French
bread. Makes 6 to 8 servings.

15

Jo Ann
One of my favorite
holiday recipes...great
for "pop-in" guests because
it's so quick & easy
to prepare.

Maple Chicken Wings

2 to 3 lbs. chicken wings
1 c. maple syrup
2/3 c. chili sauce
1/2 c. onion, finely chopped
2 T. Dijon mustard
2 t. Worcestershire sauce
1/4 to 1/2 t. red pepper flakes

Place wings in a large plastic zipping bag; set aside. Combine remaining ingredients. Reserve one cup for basting; refrigerate until ready to use. Pour remaining marinade over wings, turning to coat. Seal bag; refrigerate for 4 hours, turning occasionally. Drain and discard marinade. Place wings in a lightly greased 13"x9" baking pan. Bake, uncovered, at 375 degrees for 30 to 40 minutes, basting with reserved marinade, until golden and juices run clear when pierced. Makes 2 to 3 dozen.

Donna Nowicki
Center City, MN

The tasty maple and Dijon marinade makes these wings extra special.

Creamy BLT Dip

Barbara Thurman
Carlyle, IL
Put the "L" in BLT!
Simply spoon dip into
a hollowed-out head of
lettuce for serving.

1 lb. bacon, crisply cooked
    and crumbled
1 c. mayonnaise
1 c. sour cream
2 tomatoes, chopped
Optional: chopped fresh chives

Blend together bacon, mayonnaise
and sour cream; chill. Stir in tomatoes
just before serving; sprinkle with
chives, if desired. Makes 2-1/2 cups.

Herbed Bagel Chips:

butter-flavored non-stick
    vegetable spray
9 frozen mini bagels, thawed
1-1/2 t. Italian seasoning
1/4 t. onion powder
1/4 t. garlic powder
1/8 t. cayenne pepper

Spray a baking sheet lightly with
vegetable spray; set aside. Slice each
bagel horizontally into 4 slices; place
in a single layer on baking sheet. Spray
bagel slices lightly with vegetable
spray. Combine spices in a jar with
a shaker lid; sprinkle over chips.
Bake at 375 degrees for 12 minutes,
or until crisp. Makes 3 dozen.

17

Mini Sausage Tarts

1 lb. ground pork sausage,
  browned and drained
8-oz. pkg. shredded Mexican-
  blend cheese
3/4 c. ranch salad dressing
2 T. black olives, chopped
4 pkgs. 15-count frozen
  mini phyllo cups
Optional: diced red pepper,
  diced black olives

Combine sausage, cheese, salad
dressing and olives; blend well.
Divide among phyllo cups; arrange
on ungreased baking sheets. If desired,
sprinkle with diced pepper and black
olives. Bake at 350 degrees for 10 to
12 minutes. Makes 5 dozen.

Wanda Boykin
Lewisburg, TN

These look so fancy on an
appetizer tray...and your
friends will never know
how easy they are to make!

Pizza Fondue

1 lb. ground beef
1 onion, chopped
2 10-oz. cans pizza sauce
1 T. cornstarch
1-1/2 t. fennel seed
1-1/2 t. dried oregano
1/4 t. garlic powder
2-1/2 c. shredded Cheddar
   cheese
2 c. shredded Mozzarella cheese
2 loaves French bread, sliced
   and toasted

Brown ground beef and onion in
a skillet over medium heat; drain.
Add remaining ingredients except
bread; simmer until cheese melts.
Serve hot with bread slices for
dipping. Serves 6 to 8.

19

Michelle Golz
Freeport, IL

Keep warm in a fondue
pot or simmering on low
in a slow cooker.

Party Nibblers

1 c. cashews
1 c. peanuts
1 c. bite-size cheese crackers
1 c. bite-size shredded wheat
  cereal squares
1 c. bite-size shredded rice
  cereal squares
1 c. mini pretzels
2 T. grated Parmesan cheese
1/3 c. butter, melted
1 t. Worcestershire sauce
1/2 t. celery salt
1/2 t. garlic powder

Combine nuts, crackers, cereals and pretzels in a large bowl; mix well and set aside. Whisk remaining ingredients together in a small bowl; pour over mix, tossing to coat. Spread in an ungreased 15"x10" jelly-roll pan; bake at 350 degrees for 15 to 20 minutes, stirring often. Cool completely; store in an airtight container. Makes 6 cups.

Linda Mills
Pasadena, MD

Send a plastic zipping bag filled with Party Nibblers to your favorite college student...a welcome gift!

Summer Sparkle

48-oz. bottle ruby red
  grapefruit juice
12-oz. can frozen orange juice
  concentrate, thawed
6-oz. can frozen lemonade
  concentrate, thawed
2-ltr. bottle lemon-lime soda,
  chilled
Optional: lemon slices, fresh
  mint sprigs

Stir together grapefruit juice,
orange juice concentrate and
lemonade concentrate in a gallon
pitcher; refrigerate until chilled.
At serving time, stir in soda; garnish
as desired. Makes 16 to 20 servings.

21

Eleanor Bamford
Boonton, NJ
Serve in tall fluted
glasses with lots of ice...
oh-so refreshing!

Tangy Meatballs

2 lbs. ground beef
2 eggs, beaten
1/2 t. salt
3/4 c. quick-cooking oats,
  uncooked
1-1/3 c. chili sauce, divided
1/2 c. grape jelly
Optional: dried parsley

Combine ground beef, eggs, salt, oats
and 1/3 cup chili sauce. Shape into
one-inch balls; place in an ungreased
shallow baking pan. Bake at 400 degrees
for 15 to 17 minutes; drain. Combine
grape jelly and remaining chili sauce
in a large saucepan; cover and cook
over medium heat, stirring occasionally
until mixture is well blended. Add
meatballs and continue cooking until
heated through. Sprinkle with parsley,
if desired. Makes 5 dozen.

Charlotte Smith
Huntingdon, PA
Grape jelly and chili
sauce team up to
create a surprisingly
zingy sauce.

Cheddar-Chive Bites

2-1/2 c. biscuit baking mix
1 c. shredded Cheddar cheese
3/4 c. milk
1/8 t. garlic powder
6 T. butter, melted and divided
3 T. fresh chives, snipped and
   divided
2 5-oz. containers garlic & herb
   cheese spread, softened
Garnish: thinly sliced cucumber
   and radish

23

Combine baking mix, cheese,
milk, garlic powder and
2 tablespoons butter; mix well.
Drop by tablespoonfuls onto
ungreased baking sheets. Bake at
400 degrees for 10 to 12 minutes,
just until golden. Mix remaining
butter and one tablespoon chives;
brush over warm biscuits. Split
biscuits; set aside. Blend cheese
spread and remaining chives. Spread
lightly onto bottom halves of biscuits;
add cucumber, radish and top halves.
Makes 2 to 3 dozen.

Jean Martin
Hingham, MA
I keep a pot of fresh
chives in the kitchen
windowsill just so I can
make these year 'round.

Dried Beef Cheese Ball

2 8-oz. pkgs. cream cheese,
   softened
1 c. shredded Cheddar cheese
2-1/2 oz. pkg. dried beef, finely
   chopped and divided
3 T. green onion, chopped
2 to 3 T. mayonnaise-style
   salad dressing
1 t. Worcestershire sauce
1/2 c. chopped walnuts
assorted snack crackers

Combine all ingredients except
walnuts and crackers, setting aside
1/4 cup chopped beef. Blend well
and form into a ball. Mix nuts and
reserved beef; roll cheese ball in
mixture to coat. Wrap in plastic wrap;
chill 3 to 4 hours. Serve with crackers.
Makes one cheese ball.

Sharon Hall
Delaware, OH

My famous "secret
ingredient" recipe
for the yummiest
cheese ball ever!

Hot Crab Spread

2 8-oz. pkgs. cream cheese,
   softened
16-oz. can refrigerated
   pasteurized crabmeat,
   drained and flaked
2 T. green onion, finely
   chopped
1/2 c. prepared horseradish
1/2 c. sliced almonds
paprika to taste

Beat cream cheese until smooth;
blend in crabmeat, onion and
horseradish. Spread in an ungreased
one-quart casserole dish. Top with
almonds and sprinkle with paprika.
Bake, uncovered, at 375 degrees for
20 minutes. Makes about 4 cups.

25

Kara Allison
Dublin, OH

If you like seafood,
you'll really go for this
creamy, crabby spread.

Warm Blue Cheese & Bacon Dip

1/2 lb. bacon
4 cloves garlic, minced
2 8-oz. pkgs. cream cheese,
  softened
1/2 c. half-and-half
2 4-oz. containers crumbled
  blue cheese
1/4 c. fresh chives, snipped
baguette slices, celery stalks

In a skillet over medium heat, cook bacon until crisp. Drain bacon on paper towels. Add garlic to drippings in skillet; sauté until soft, about one minute. Beat together cream cheese and half-and-half with an electric mixer on high speed. Stir in crumbled bacon, garlic, blue cheese and chives; spoon into an ungreased 8"x8" baking pan. Cover and bake at 350 degrees for about 30 minutes, until lightly golden. Serve with baguette slices and celery stalks. Serves 12.

Janet Schaeper
Pickerington, OH

Garnish with a sprinkle
of extra chives
and crispy bacon...
irresistible!

Artichoke Party Triangles

16-oz. pkg. frozen phyllo dough, thawed
1/4 to 1/2 c. butter, melted
2 6-oz. jars marinated artichoke hearts, drained and chopped
10-oz. pkg. frozen chopped spinach, thawed and drained
1 clove garlic, minced
1/2 c. mayonnaise
1/2 c. sour cream
3/4 c. grated Parmesan cheese

Lay out one sheet phyllo dough on a lightly floured surface; brush lightly with butter. Layer with 4 more sheets, brushing each with butter. Cut layered dough into sixteen 3-inch squares. For filling, combine remaining ingredients; mix well. Spoon one teaspoon filling into the center of each square. Fold squares over to form triangles; crimp edges with a fork. Arrange on an ungreased baking sheet; bake at 350 degrees for 5 to 7 minutes, until golden. Makes 16.

27

Phyllis Wittig
Lancaster, CA
These crisp spinach-filled treats never last long!

Italian Sausage & Vegetable Soup

1/2 lb. Italian ground pork sausage
1 onion, finely chopped
1 clove garlic, minced
3 14-oz. cans chicken broth
1/2 c. white wine or chicken broth
28-oz. can crushed tomatoes in
    tomato purée
2 zucchini, quartered lengthwise
    and sliced
2 carrots, peeled and diced
3 stalks celery, diced
1 green pepper, diced
1 t. dried basil
1/2 t. dried oregano
1/2 c. orzo pasta, uncooked
1/2 t. salt
1/2 t. pepper

Brown sausage in a Dutch oven over medium heat. Drain, leaving a small amount of drippings in pan. Add onion and garlic; cook just until tender. Add broth, wine or broth, vegetables and herbs; bring to a boil. Add uncooked pasta; reduce heat and simmer for 20 minutes, until vegetables and pasta are tender. Add salt and pepper to taste. Makes 6 to 8 servings.

Kate Sanderson
Chicago, IL
A great make-ahead recipe...
even more flavorful when
reheated. Garnish with
freshly shredded Parmesan.

Oven Beef & Noodles

1-1/2 oz. pkg. onion soup mix
4 c. water
10-3/4 oz. can cream of
   mushroom soup
3-lb. boneless beef chuck roast
12-oz. pkg. kluski egg noodles,
   uncooked

Combine soup mix and water in a roasting pan; stir in soup. Place roast in pan on top of soup mixture. Cover and bake at 350 degrees for 4 hours, or until meat is very tender. Remove roast from pan and shred; return to pan. Add noodles to pan; reduce heat to 300 degrees. Cover and bake for 20 to 30 minutes, stirring every 15 minutes until noodles are tender. Add water if necessary to prevent drying out. Makes 6 to 8 servings.

29

Kristie Rigo
Friedens, PA
A hearty stick-to-your-ribs dish we all crave on cold winter days.

Best-Ever Grilled Cheese Sandwiches

3-oz. pkg. cream cheese, softened
3/4 c. mayonnaise-type salad
  dressing
1 c. shredded mozzarella cheese
1 c. shredded Cheddar cheese
1/4 t. garlic powder
1/8 t. seasoned salt
8 to 10 slices white bread
2 T. butter, softened

Blend cream cheese and salad dressing until smooth; stir in cheeses, garlic powder and salt. Spread half the bread slices with cheese mixture. Top with remaining bread; spread butter on both sides of sandwiches. Grill in a skillet over medium heat until golden on both sides. Makes 4 to 5 sandwiches.

Beth Parrish
Linn, MO

We love this rich, cheesy spread on thick slices of bakery-fresh sourdough or Italian bread.

Creamy Tomato Soup

1 onion, chopped
2 T. margarine
2 14-1/2 oz. cans diced tomatoes
2 10-3/4 oz. cans tomato soup
1-1/2 c. milk
1 t. sugar
1/2 t. dried basil
1/2 t. paprika
1/8 t. garlic powder
8-oz. pkg. cream cheese,
    cubed and softened
Optional: croutons

In a large saucepan over medium
heat, sauté onion in margarine
until tender. Stir in remaining
ingredients except cream cheese
and croutons; bring to a boil.
Reduce heat; cover and simmer for
10 minutes. Stir in cream cheese and
heat until melted. Serve immediately,
garnished with croutons if desired.
Makes 8 servings.

Flo Burtnett
Gage, OK

The perfect partner
for a grilled
cheese sandwich!

Broccoli-Cheddar Soup

3/4 c. onion, finely chopped
3/4 c. butter
3/4 c. all-purpose flour
1 t. salt
1 t. pepper
3 c. chicken broth
4-1/2 c. milk
3 c. broccoli, chopped and cooked
3/4 c. shredded Cheddar cheese

In a large saucepan over medium heat, sauté onion in butter until tender. Stir in flour, salt and pepper; cook and stir until smooth and bubbly. Add broth and milk all at once. Cook and stir until mixture thickens and boils; add broccoli. Reduce heat and simmer, stirring constantly, until heated through. Remove from heat; stir in cheese until melted. Serves 6.

Donna Nowicki
Center City, MN

Just add warm, crusty bread for a hearty, complete meal...so comforting on a chilly evening.

Stacie's Spaghetti Pie

8-oz. pkg. spaghetti, cooked
2 t. olive oil
1 c. favorite pasta sauce
1 c. sliced mushrooms
1/2 c. green pepper, chopped
1/2 c. black olives, chopped
1/4 lb. mozzarella cheese, cubed
2 t. garlic, minced
1/2 t. Italian seasoning
1/2 t. seasoning salt
1/4 t. red pepper flakes
4 eggs
1/2 c. milk
3/4 c. sliced pepperoni
1/2 c. grated Parmesan cheese

Toss cooked spaghetti with oil in a large bowl; add sauce, vegetables, mozzarella, garlic and seasonings. Mix well; spread in a lightly greased 13"x9" baking pan. Whisk together eggs and milk; pour over spaghetti mixture. Arrange pepperoni evenly on top; sprinkle with Parmesan. Bake, uncovered, at 375 degrees for 25 to 30 minutes, until bubbly and golden. Let stand for 5 minutes; cut into squares. Makes 6 to 8 servings.

Stacie Mickley
Gooseberry Patch

Everyone loves spaghetti! This baked version makes it ideal for toting to a potluck with friends.

Make-Ahead Brunch Casserole

1 T. butter
2 onions, chopped
2 c. sliced mushrooms
4 c. frozen shredded hashbrowns,
   thawed
salt and pepper to taste
1/4 t. garlic salt
1 lb. bacon, crisply cooked and
   crumbled
4 eggs
1-1/2 c. milk
1/8 t. dried parsley
1 c. shredded Cheddar cheese

Melt butter in a skillet. Sauté onions
and mushrooms until tender; set
aside. Spread hashbrowns in a greased
13"x9" baking pan. Sprinkle with salt,
pepper and garlic salt; top with bacon,
onions and mushrooms. Whisk together
eggs with milk and parsley; pour over
casserole and top with cheese. Cover
and refrigerate overnight. Bake,
uncovered, at 400 degrees for one hour,
or until set. Makes 4 to 6 servings.

Kelly Dalton
Lewisburg, TN

Assemble this casserole
the night before...in the
morning, just pop it in
the oven. What a time-saver!

Classic Tuna Noodle Casserole

16-oz. pkg. wide egg noodles,
   cooked
2 10-3/4 oz. cans cream of
   mushroom soup
2 6-oz. cans tuna, drained
1 c. frozen peas, thawed
4-oz. can sliced mushrooms,
   drained
1 to 2 c. milk
salt and pepper to taste
8-oz. pkg. shredded Cheddar
   cheese
4 slices bread, toasted and
   cubed
2 T. butter, melted

Combine noodles, soup, tuna, peas
and mushrooms; stir in enough milk
to moisten well. Add salt and pepper
to taste. Spread in a lightly greased
13"x9" baking pan; sprinkle with
cheese and set aside. Toss together
bread cubes and butter; sprinkle
over top. Bake, uncovered, at
350 degrees for 25 minutes, until
hot and bubbly. Serves 6.

**Emma Wiliams
Salyersville, KY**

One taste and it's easy
to see why this was
a regular on Mom's
dinner table.

35

Veggie Patch Stew

3 zucchini, sliced
3 yellow squash, sliced
2 onions, chopped
2 tomatoes, chopped
1 eggplant, peeled and cubed
1 green pepper, chopped
1 clove garlic, minced
2 T. butter, softened
1 t. hot pepper sauce
1/2 t. curry powder
1 t. chili powder
salt and pepper to taste
Garnish: shredded mozzarella
   cheese

Place all vegetables in a large Dutch
oven over low heat. Stir in remaining
ingredients except cheese. Cover
and simmer for one hour, stirring
frequently. Do not add any liquid, as
vegetables make their own juice. Top
portions with cheese before serving.
Makes 6 servings.

Nancy Campbell
Bellingham, WA

A family favorite, made
with fresh veggies from
our summer garden.

Hearty Ham & Rice Bake

2 10-3/4 oz. cans cream of
  celery soup
1 c. light cream
1 c. shredded sharp Cheddar
  cheese
1/3 c. grated Parmesan cheese
1-1/2 T. onion, grated
1 T. mustard
1/3 t. pepper
4 c. cooked rice
4 c. cooked ham, cubed
16-oz. can green beans,
  drained
6-oz. can French fried onions

Combine soup and cream in a large
bowl; stir in cheeses, onion, mustard
and pepper. Add rice, ham and
beans; turn into a lightly greased
3-quart casserole dish. Sprinkle
with onions. Bake, uncovered,
at 350 degrees for one hour.
Serves 10.

37

Terees Grippe
Mukilteo, WA

My "old reliable" recipe
when I want my family &
friends to have a full
tummy and a big smile!

Shepherd's Pie

2 lbs. ground beef
1/2 onion, chopped
garlic powder and seasoning salt
   to taste
.75-oz. pkg. brown gravy mix
2 10-3/4 oz. cans cream of
   mushroom soup
2-1/2 c. water
1-1/2 c. frozen sliced carrots,
   thawed
10-oz. pkg. frozen peas, thawed
salt and pepper to taste
2-1/2 to 3 c. potatoes, peeled,
   cooked and mashed
paprika to taste

Brown beef and onion in a skillet; season to taste with garlic powder and seasoning salt. Drain; pour into a large bowl. Stir in gravy mix, soup, water, carrots and peas; mix well. Spoon into a greased 13"x 9" baking pan or 9" deep-dish pie plate; sprinkle with salt and pepper. Spread mashed potatoes over top; bake at 350 degrees for 45 minutes. Sprinkle with paprika. Makes 4 to 6 servings.

Kimberly Pfleiderer
Galion, OH

Stir in other veggies
if you like...corn
and baby limas are
tasty additions.

Baked Steak with Gravy

1 c. all-purpose flour
1/8 t. salt
1/8 t. pepper
6 to 8 beef cube steaks
1 t. butter
2 10-3/4 oz. cans golden
   mushroom soup
2-1/2 c. water
4-oz. can sliced mushrooms,
   drained

Mix flour, salt and pepper in a
shallow bowl. Dredge steaks in
flour mixture. Melt butter in
a skillet over medium heat; add steaks
and brown on both sides. Arrange
steaks in a lightly greased 13"x9"
baking pan; set aside. Combine soup,
water and mushrooms. Pour soup
mixture over steaks; cover with
aluminum foil. Bake at 325 degrees
for 45 to 50 minutes. Uncover;
bake an additional 15 minutes.
Serves 6 to 8.

39

Amy Halstead
Winfield, WV

As a wedding gift, a dear
friend hand-copied 75 of
her tried & true recipes
for me...this is one of
the very best.

Buttermilk Fried Chicken

1/2 c. all-purpose flour
1 T. fresh parsley, chopped
1 T. fresh thyme, chopped
1 t. salt
1/2 t. garlic powder
1/4 t. pepper
1 c. buttermilk
3 to 3-1/2 lbs. chicken
1/4 c. oil
1/4 c. butter-flavored shortening

Combine flour, herbs and seasonings in a shallow dish; pour buttermilk into a separate shallow dish. Dip chicken in buttermilk; turn in flour mixture to coat and set aside. Heat oil and shortening in a large skillet; add chicken, skin-side down. Cook over medium-high heat, turning occasionally, until golden and juices run clear, about 35 to 45 minutes. Serves 6.

Robyn Burton
Maryvale, TN
Delicious served fresh and hot...and for a picnic, there's nothing better than cold fried chicken!

Crunchy Hot Chicken Salad

6 T. butter, divided
1 c. celery, chopped
1/2 c. green pepper, diced
1/3 c. onion, chopped
2 to 3 T. pimentos, diced
4-oz. can sliced mushrooms,
    drained
2-1/4 oz. pkg. slivered almonds
4 c. cooked chicken, diced
1 c. mayonnaise
10-3/4 oz. can cream of
    celery soup
1 t. salt
1 c. corn flake cereal,
    crushed

Melt 4 tablespoons butter in a large
skillet over medium heat; add
vegetables and almonds. Sauté
until vegetables are tender; spoon
into an ungreased 13"x9" baking
pan. Add chicken, mayonnaise,
soup and salt; mix well. Melt
remaining butter and toss with
cereal; sprinkle over top. Bake,
uncovered, at 350 degrees for
30 minutes. Makes 10 servings.

41

Lynne Davisson
Cable, OH
Serve with tropical
fruit cups for a
delightful luncheon.

BBQ Chicken Pizza

12-inch Italian pizza crust
3 c. cooked chicken, shredded
1 c. barbecue sauce
1 c. shredded mozzarella cheese
1/2 c. shredded Cheddar cheese

Place pizza crust on a lightly greased
12" round pizza pan. Combine chicken
and barbecue sauce; spread on pizza
crust. Sprinkle with cheeses. Bake
at 450 degrees for 8 to 10 minutes,
or until cheeses melt and crust is
crisp. Serves 4.

Ginny Bone
Saint Peters, MO

With only 5 ingredients,
this is a scrumptious
hurry-up meal your family
will absolutely love.

Slow-Cooker Sloppy Joes

1-1/2 lbs. ground beef
1 c. onion, chopped
2 cloves garlic, minced
3/4 c. catsup
1/2 c. green pepper, chopped
1/2 c. celery, chopped
1/4 c. water
1 T. brown sugar, packed
2 T. mustard
2 T. vinegar
2 T. Worcestershire sauce
1-1/2 t. chili powder
6 to 8 hamburger buns,
    toasted
Optional: pickle slices

In a skillet over medium heat, brown beef, onion and garlic; drain and set aside. Combine remaining ingredients except buns and pickle slices in a slow cooker; stir in beef mixture. Cover; cook on low setting for 6 to 8 hours. Spoon onto buns; garnish with pickle slices, if desired. Serves 6 to 8.

43

Denise Oravecz
Pittsburgh, PA
Start this in the morning,
then relax...dinner will
be ready when you are!

Tex-Mex Meatball Subs

1-1/2 lbs. ground beef
1 egg, beaten
1 c. tortilla chips, crushed
1-1/4 oz. pkg. taco seasoning mix,
    divided
16-oz. jar salsa, divided
26-oz. jar spaghetti sauce
8 hoagie or sub buns, split
1 lb. Monterey Jack cheese, sliced
Optional: lettuce, jalapeño
    peppers

Mix together ground beef, egg, chips,
half of taco seasoning and one cup
salsa. Form into one-inch balls; place
in an ungreased 13"x9" baking pan.
Bake at 375 degrees for 45 minutes;
remove from oven and drain. Combine
spaghetti sauce, remaining salsa and
remaining taco seasoning in a
saucepan. Simmer for several minutes
over low heat; pour over meatballs.
Spoon meatballs onto buns; top with
cheese slices. Garnish with lettuce
and jalapeño peppers, if desired.
Makes 8 sandwiches.

Tammy Rowe
Bellevue, OH
Just for fun, serve in
paper napkin-lined baskets
with chips and a pickle.

Taco Soup

1-1/2 lbs. ground beef
1 onion, chopped
2 16-oz. cans kidney beans,
    drained
16-oz. can black beans, drained
16-oz. can pinto beans, drained
15-oz. can corn, drained
14-1/2 oz. can diced tomatoes
14-1/2 oz. can stewed tomatoes
3.8-oz. can sliced black olives,
    drained and diced
30-oz. can tomato juice
1-1/2 oz. pkg. taco seasoning
    mix
salt and pepper to taste
Garnish: sour cream, tortilla
    strips, sliced black olives,
    sliced green onions

Brown beef and onion in a skillet.
Drain; combine with remaining
ingredients in a large stockpot. Bring
to a boil over medium heat; reduce
heat and simmer for 30 minutes.
Garnish individual portions as
desired. Serves 8 to 10.

45

Linda Turner
Tucson, AZ

A handy mix makes sure
this hearty soup is
seasoned just right
every time.

Great American Submarine

1-lb. loaf Italian bread, halved
    horizontally
1/2 c. mayonnaise
1/2 lb. deli honey ham, thinly
    sliced
1/2 lb. salami, thinly sliced
1 tomato, thinly sliced
1 onion, thinly sliced
1 green pepper, thinly sliced
1/2 lb. Muenster cheese, sliced
2 3.8-oz. cans sliced black
    olives, drained
2 banana peppers, seeded
    and sliced
1 bunch leaf lettuce, torn
salt and pepper to taste

Spread bottom half of loaf with
mayonnaise. Layer remaining
ingredients in order given; top with
remaining half of loaf. Slice and
serve. Makes 4 servings.

Margie Schaffner
Altoona, IA
Celebrate the 4th of July
with flags, food and fun!
This oversize sandwich
is picnic-perfect.

Bacon & Blue Cheese Stuffed Burgers

1-1/2 lbs. ground beef
1 T. Worcestershire sauce
2 T. Dijon mustard
1/2 t. pepper
4 to 6 slices bacon, crisply
  cooked and crumbled
4-oz. container crumbled
  blue cheese
4 hamburger buns, split and
  toasted
Garnish: sliced red onion,
  sliced tomato, lettuce leaves

47

Combine ground beef, Worcestershire
sauce, mustard and pepper. Mix
lightly and form into eight, 1/4-inch
thick patties. Stir together bacon and
blue cheese; set aside 1/3 of mixture
for topping. Spoon remaining mixture
onto centers of 4 patties. Top with
remaining 4 patties; press edges
together to seal. Grill over medium-
high high heat to desired doneness,
4 to 6 minutes per side, topping with
reserved bacon mixture when nearly
done. Serve burgers on toasted rolls,
garnished as desired. Makes 4 burgers.

Tom Gullette
Houston, TX

Packed with savory
flavors...these aren't
your ordinary burgers
on the grill!

Marvelous Meatloaf

3/4 c. bread crumbs
3/4 c. milk
1-1/2 lbs. ground beef
1 onion, chopped
1 T. salt, or to taste
1 T. pepper, or to taste
1 T. Worcestershire sauce
1/2 c. catsup
2 T. mustard
2 T. brown sugar, packed

Combine bread crumbs and milk in a large bowl. Add ground beef, onion, salt, pepper and sauce; mix well. Shape into a loaf and place in an ungreased 9"x5" loaf pan. Stir catsup, mustard and brown sugar together; spoon over meatloaf. Bake, uncovered, at 375 degrees for one hour. Makes 8 servings.

Amy Herman
Orlando, FL

Thick slices served with mashed potatoes...now, that's comfort food!

Sunday Chicken & Dressing

10-3/4 oz. can cream of chicken
 soup
10-3/4 oz. can cream of celery
 or cream of mushroom soup
1 c. chicken broth
2-1/2 to 3 lbs. cooked chicken,
 cubed
2 6-oz. pkgs. chicken-flavored
 stuffing mix, prepared

Combine soups and broth in
a large bowl; set aside. Place half
of chicken in a lightly greased
13"x9" baking pan; top with half of
stuffing and half of soup mixture.
Repeat layers, ending with soup
mixture. Bake, uncovered, at
350 degrees for one hour.
Makes 10 servings.

49

Laura Strausberger
Roswell, GA

So good! Try it with
leftover turkey too.

Rosemary Roast Pork Loin

3-lb. boneless pork loin roast
2 t. dried rosemary
2 t. dry mustard
1 t. ground ginger
1 t. salt
1 t. pepper
2 T. olive oil
6 cloves garlic, minced

Place roast in an ungreased shallow roasting pan; set aside. Crush together seasonings in a mortar and pestle. Add oil and garlic to make a paste. Spread mixture over roast; let stand at room temperature for 30 to 45 minutes. Bake, uncovered, at 350 degrees for one to 1-1/2 hours. Let stand 15 to 20 minutes before slicing. Makes 6 to 8 servings.

Rachael Leonardis
Katy, TX

So juicy and tender...our favorite way to enjoy pork roast.

Easy Pork & Sauerkraut

1 lb. boneless pork roast, cubed
32-oz. jar sauerkraut
12-oz. bottle beer or
　　non-alcoholic beer
1/2 apple, cored and peeled
1 T. garlic, minced
2 t. dill weed
1 t. onion salt
1 t. dry mustard

Combine all ingredients in a slow cooker; stir well. Cover and cook on high setting for one hour. Reduce to low setting and continue cooking for 5 hours, or until pork is cooked through. Discard apple before serving. Serves 4 to 6.

51

Carrie Knotts
Kalispell, MT
A must-have on New Year's Day! It's easy to double for heartier appetites too.

Creamy Chicken Enchiladas

2 c. cooked chicken, shredded
1 c. green pepper, diced
16-oz. jar picante sauce, divided
8-oz. pkg. cream cheese, softened
10 8-inch flour tortillas
16-oz. pkg. Mexican pasteurized
    process cheese spread, cubed
1/4 c. milk
2 2-1/4 oz. cans sliced black
    olives, drained
Garnish: salsa, guacamole,
    sour cream

In a skillet over low heat, cook and stir chicken, green pepper, one cup picante sauce and cream cheese until smooth. Spoon 1/4 cup of mixture onto each tortilla. Roll up and place seam-side down in an ungreased 13"x9" baking pan. In same skillet, cook cubed cheese spread and milk over low heat until melted and smooth; pour over enchiladas. Sprinkle olives on top; spoon remaining picante sauce over enchiladas. Cover with aluminum foil. Bake at 350 degrees for 25 minutes, until heated through. Serve with salsa, guacamole and sour cream on the side. Makes 10 servings.

Frances Cummons
Lakeview, OH

Pick up a roasted deli chicken to jump-start this yummy dinner favorite.

Vickie's Shredded Chicken Sandwiches

4 T. olive oil
4 boneless, skinless chicken
   breasts
1 onion, chopped
10-3/4 oz. can cream of
   mushroom soup
1 c. chicken broth
2 t. soy sauce
2 t. Worcestershire sauce
1/2 c. sherry or chicken broth
salt and pepper to taste
8 sandwich buns, split
Optional: pickle slices,
   lettuce leaves

Heat oil in a skillet over medium-high heat. Brown chicken for 5 minutes on each side. Place chicken in a slow cooker; set aside. Add onion to skillet; sauté until golden. Add soup, broth, sauces, sherry or broth, salt and pepper to skillet; stir well and pour over chicken in slow cooker. Cover and cook on low setting for 6 to 8 hours. Shred chicken with a fork; spoon onto buns. Garnish with pickles and lettuce, if desired. Makes 8 sandwiches.

53

Vickie
Tender chicken piled high on a soft bun... just like the sandwiches at old-fashioned church socials.

Scalloped Potatoes & Ham

2 T. onion, chopped
1/4 c. butter
1/4 c. all-purpose flour
1/2 t. dry mustard
1 t. salt
1/8 t. pepper
1-1/2 c. milk
2 c. shredded Cheddar cheese,
    divided
6 c. potatoes, peeled, cooked
    and sliced
1/2 lb. cooked ham, cubed

In a skillet over medium heat, sauté onion in butter; blend in flour, mustard, salt and pepper. Gradually add milk, stirring constantly until thickened; mix in 1-1/2 cups cheese and stir until melted. Remove from heat; add potatoes and toss to coat. Spoon into a greased 13"x9" baking dish; arrange ham and remaining cheese on top. Bake, uncovered, at 350 degrees for 30 minutes, until hot and bubbly. Serves 6.

Lisa Quick
Clarksburg, MD
Filled with melted cheese and potatoes, this is one of those casseroles everyone loves.

Quick & Spicy Shrimp Linguine

2 T. butter
2 cloves garlic, minced
14-1/2 oz. can spicy stewed
    tomatoes
1 lb. cooked, peeled large shrimp
1 red pepper, diced
2 green onions, chopped
8-oz. pkg. linguine pasta,
    cooked
Garnish: grated Parmesan
    cheese

55

Melt butter over medium heat in
a large skillet. Add garlic; cook
until golden, about one minute.
Add tomatoes with juice; bring to
a boil. Simmer uncovered, stirring
occasionally, for 10 minutes, or
until slightly thickened. Add shrimp,
red pepper and green onions; cook
for 5 minutes, until shrimp is
heated through. Stir in hot pasta;
toss until well coated. Garnish with
Parmesan cheese. Serves 4.

Laurel Perry
Loganville, GA

Impress your
family & friends with
this easy-to-sauté
classic recipe.

Mexicalli Pie

1 lb. ground beef
1/2 c. onion, chopped
1/2 c. green pepper, chopped
1-1/2 c. frozen corn, thawed
  and drained
1 c. chunky-style zesty salsa
3/4 c. shredded sharp or
  Mexican-style Cheddar cheese
1/8 t. pepper
1 c. corn chips, crushed
Optional: sour cream, sliced
  jalapeño peppers, diced tomato

Brown beef, onion and pepper in a skillet; drain. Add corn, salsa, Cheddar cheese and pepper. Place beef mixture in a lightly greased 10" pie plate; top with crushed chips. Bake at 350 degrees for 30 minutes. Let cool for 10 minutes; garnish as desired. Serves 6 to 8.

Carol Huck
Chester, NJ
A side of Spanish rice will complete this dinner nicely.

Barbecued Pork Chops

8 pork chops
3 T. oil
1/2 c. catsup
1/3 c. vinegar
1 c. water
1 t. salt
1 t. celery seed
1/2 t. nutmeg
1 bay leaf

In a large skillet over medium heat, brown chops in oil. Drain; arrange chops in a greased 13"x9" baking pan. Combine remaining ingredients and pour over chops. Cover with aluminum foil. Bake at 325 degrees for 1-1/2 hours, until tender. Discard bay leaf before serving. Makes 8 servings.

Sandra Seymour
Taylor, MI

Pop this in the oven on a leisurely Sunday afternoon...it practically fixes itself!

Heartland Barbecued Beef

2-lb. beef chuck roast, cut
   crosswise into 1/2-inch slices
1/2 c. onion, chopped
2 cloves garlic, minced
2 c. catsup
1/4 c. brown sugar, packed
1/4 c. Worcestershire sauce
1 t. mustard
1/2 t. salt
1/4 t. pepper
6 to 8 onion buns, split

Combine all ingredients except buns in
a slow cooker; mix well. Cover and
cook on low setting for 6 to 8 hours,
stirring occasionally, until meat is
tender. Serve on buns. Makes 6 to
8 sandwiches.

Sharon Crider
Junction City, KS

Make 'em mini! Spoon
onto small dinner rolls
for a fun-to-eat
party snack.

Country Beef Roast

2 T. all-purpose flour
3 to 5-lb. beef chuck roast
1-1/2 oz. pkg. onion soup mix
10-3/4 oz. can cream of
    mushroom soup
1-1/4 c. water
6 to 8 potatoes, peeled and
    cubed
3 to 4 onions, sliced
4 to 6 carrots, peeled and sliced

59

Shake flour in a large oven bag.
Arrange bag in a roasting pan;
place roast into bag. Mix together
soup mix, mushroom soup and
water; spread over roast. Close bag
with nylon tie provided; cut six,
1/2-inch slits in top. Bake at
325 degrees for 3 to 4 hours, until
roast is fork-tender. Add vegetables to
bag; reclose bag and bake an additional
hour. Serve with pan drippings as
gravy. Serves 10 to 12.

Mylissa Gholson
Aspermont, TX

I like to fix this
delicious meal and leave
it roasting in the oven
while I'm out in the barn.

Harvest Spinach Salad

1 bunch fresh spinach,
  stems removed
5 slices bacon, crisply cooked
  and crumbled
5 green onions, sliced
1/2 c. sliced almonds
1 Red Delicious apple, cored and
  thinly sliced
1/4 lb. Monterey Jack cheese,
  cubed
1/4 c. olive oil
3 T. white wine vinegar
1 t. sugar
1/2 t. dry mustard

Toss together spinach, bacon, green
onions, almonds, apple and cheese in a
large salad bowl. In a small bowl, whisk
together olive oil, vinegar, sugar and
mustard. Toss dressing with salad; serve
immediately. Makes 4 to 6 servings.

Barb Bargdill
Gooseberry Patch

Top with sliced, grilled
chicken to turn this
flavorful salad into a
satisfying light meal.

Mom's Applesauce Muffins

1/2 c. butter, softened
1 c. sugar
1 egg, beaten
1 c. applesauce
1 t. cinnamon
1/2 t. ground cloves
1 t. baking soda
1/4 t. salt
2 c. all-purpose flour
1 c. raisins

Combine all ingredients; stir until moistened. Fill lightly greased muffin cups 3/4 full; sprinkle with Crumb Topping. Bake at 350 degrees for 25 to 30 minutes. Makes 12 to 16 muffins.

Crumb Topping:

1/2 c. butter
3/4 c. all-purpose flour
3/4 c. quick-cooking oats, uncooked
1/2 c. brown sugar, packed
2 t. cinnamon

Blend all ingredients until crumbly.

Emily Johnson
Pocatello, ID

Fill your kitchen with the delectable aroma of apples and cinnamon.

61

Brocco-Flower Salad

1 c. mayonnaise
2 T. red wine vinegar
1/3 c. sugar
1/2 head broccoli, cut into
 flowerets
1/2 head cauliflower, cut into
 flowerets
1/2 c. chopped pecans
1/2 c. red onion, chopped
1/2 c. raisins
8 to 10 slices bacon, crisply
 cooked and crumbled

Combine mayonnaise, vinegar and
sugar; cover and chill. Combine
remaining ingredients in a large bowl.
Add mayonnaise mixture. Mix well
and chill before serving. Serves 6.

Sandie Pfeiffer
Montpelier, VA

Fresh broccoli combines
with cauliflower for this
crunchy treat...raisins add
just a hint of sweetness.

Greek Pasta Salad

8-oz. pkg. elbow macaroni,
  cooked
1/2 lb. sliced mushrooms
15 cherry tomatoes, halved
1 c. yellow or red pepper, sliced
1/2 c. green onion, chopped
3/4 c. sliced black olives,
  drained
1 c. crumbled feta cheese
Optional: 3/4 c. pepperoni,
  diced

Combine all ingredients in a
large bowl. Pour dressing over
top; toss until evenly coated.
Cover and chill 2 hours to overnight.
Makes 10 to 12 servings.

Dressing:

1/2 c. olive oil
1/2 c. red wine vinegar
1-1/2 t. garlic powder
1-1/2 t. dried basil
1-1/2 t. dried oregano
3/4 t. pepper
3/4 t. sugar

Whisk together ingredients in
a small bowl.

63

Lisa Seymour
Blooming Prairie, MN
A super make-ahead
recipe for potlucks
or parties...it feeds
a crowd too!

Garlicky Parmesan Asparagus

1 T. butter
1/4 c. olive oil
2 cloves garlic, minced
1 lb. asparagus spears, trimmed
2 t. lemon juice
salt and pepper to taste
Garnish: shredded Parmesan
   cheese

Combine butter and oil in a skillet
over medium heat. Add garlic; sauté
for one to 2 minutes. Add asparagus
and cook to desired tenderness,
stirring occasionally, about 10 minutes.
Drain; sprinkle asparagus with lemon
juice, salt and pepper. Arrange on
serving platter; sprinkle with
Parmesan. Makes 4 servings.

Julie Vidovich
Winston-Salem, NC
Savor the flavor of
garden-fresh asparagus
in this simple recipe...
nice with a baked ham.

Goalpost Apple Slaw

2-1/4 c. red apples, cored
    and cubed
2-1/4 c. green apples, cored
    and cubed
1 c. coleslaw mix
1/3 c. sweetened dried
    cranberries
1/3 c. chopped walnuts
1 c. sour cream
3 T. lemon juice
1 to 2 T. vinegar
1 T. sugar
1 T. poppy seed
3/4 t. salt
1/8 t. pepper

Lightly toss ingredients in a large
bowl until well mixed. Chill for
at least one hour before serving.
Serves 6 to 8.

65

Mary Romack
Ann Arbor, MI

So crisp, cool and
crunchy...a tailgating
favorite!

Sweet Ambrosia Salad

20-oz. can pineapple chunks,
   drained
14-1/2 oz. jar maraschino cherries,
   drained
11-oz. can mandarin oranges,
   drained
8-oz. container sour cream
10-1/2 oz. pkg. pastel mini
   marshmallows
1/2 c. sweetened flaked coconut

Combine fruit in a large bowl; stir
in sour cream until coated. Fold in
marshmallows and coconut; cover and
chill overnight. Makes 8 to 10 servings.

Rachel Ripley
Pittsburgh, PA

Kids of all ages love
this sweet, creamy salad!

Fresh Tomato Pie

3 to 4 tomatoes, diced
salt and pepper to taste
1/2 c. mayonnaise
1 c. shredded sharp Cheddar
  cheese
1 c. shredded Colby Jack cheese
1 T. dried chives
1 T. dried basil
9-inch pie crust, baked

Place tomatoes between paper towels to absorb some of the moisture. Remove tomatoes to a bowl and sprinkle with salt and pepper. In a separate bowl, combine mayonnaise, cheeses, chives and basil; carefully add tomatoes. Pour mixture into pie crust. Bake at 400 degrees for 20 to 30 minutes. Makes 8 servings.

67

Lynette Edmondson
Dickson, TN
A delightful way to prepare sun-ripe tomatoes fresh from the farmstand!

Creamy Cucumber Crunch

8 cucumbers
1 t. salt
6 radishes, thinly sliced
8-oz. container plain yogurt
1/2 c. sour cream
1/2 c. fresh dill, chopped and
    loosely packed
2 T. lime juice
1/4 t. pepper
1 clove garlic, pressed

Remove several strips of peel from each cucumber; cut in half lengthwise. Scoop out seeds and thinly slice each half crosswise. Toss cucumbers with salt in a large bowl; set aside for 30 minutes. Combine remaining ingredients in a separate large bowl; mix well and set aside. Drain cucumbers, pressing to remove as much liquid as possible. Pat dry with paper towels. Add to radish mixture and toss until evenly coated. Cover and chill for at least one hour to overnight. Serves 10.

Elaine Crago
Ostrander, OH

A dreamy dressing and the satisfying crunch of fresh veggies...always a hit at summer cookouts.

Blue Cheese Potato Salad

3 lbs. new potatoes,
   quartered
1 c. mayonnaise
1 c. sour cream
2 t. lemon juice
1 bunch green onions,
   chopped
5 stalks celery, chopped
1/2 c. fresh dill, chopped
1/2 c. crumbled blue cheese
1 t. salt
pepper to taste
Optional: slivered toasted
   almonds

Cover potatoes with water in a
saucepan; bring to a boil. Simmer
until tender; drain and cool. Blend
together mayonnaise, sour cream
and lemon juice in a large bowl. Add
green onions, celery and dill; fold in
blue cheese and potatoes. Add salt
and pepper to taste; chill overnight.
If desired, garnish with almonds at
serving time. Makes 10 servings.

JoAnn

Try this recipe with
redskin potatoes...no need
to peel! Garnish with
sprigs of fresh dill.

69

Fried Green Tomatoes

1 c. all-purpose flour
2 eggs, beaten
1 c. Italian-flavored dry
   bread crumbs
1/2 c. shortening
2 to 3 green tomatoes, sliced
   1/4-inch thick
Garnish: chipotle mayonnaise,
   crumbled feta cheese

Place flour, eggs and bread crumbs in
separate small bowls. Melt shortening
in a large skillet over medium heat.
Dip each tomato slice into flour, then
eggs and lastly into bread crumbs. Place
tomato slices in skillet and cook until
golden, about 2 minutes on each side.
Reduce heat to low; cook an additional
3 minutes, or until tender. Drizzle
slices with chipotle mayonnaise;
sprinkle with crumbled feta cheese.
Serves 4 to 6.

Elizabeth Furry
Minden, NV

My favorite farmers'
market vendor gave me
this recipe.

Hot Bacon-Potato Salad

1/4 lb. bacon
3/4 c. celery, sliced
1/2 c. onion, chopped
1-1/2 T. all-purpose flour
3/4 c. water
1/3 c. vinegar
2 T. sugar
1-1/2 t. salt
1 t. mustard
1/4 t. celery seed
4 c. potatoes, peeled,
    cooked and sliced

71

Cook bacon in a skillet over medium heat until crisp. Remove bacon; crumble and set aside. Add celery and onion to drippings in skillet; cook until tender. Add remaining ingredients except potatoes; cook until thickened, stirring constantly. Fold in potatoes and bacon; heat through. Serve warm. Makes 4 to 6 servings.

Amber Erskine
Hartland, VT
This salad is just right for toting to a family reunion.

Country-Style Skillet Apples

1/3 c. butter
1/2 c. sugar
1/2 t. cinnamon
2 T. cornstarch
1 c. water
4 Golden Delicious apples, cored,
    peeled and sliced

Melt butter in a skillet over medium
heat. Stir in sugar, cinnamon and
cornstarch; mix well and stir in water.
Add apple slices. Cook over medium
heat, stirring occasionally, until
tender, about 10 minutes. Makes 4 to
6 servings.

Joanne Nagle
Ashtabula, OH

A perfect partner for
roast pork at dinner...
for grilled breakfast
sausages too!

Savory Cheese & Bacon Potatoes

2-1/2 lbs. Yukon Gold potatoes,
   peeled and quartered
3 T. butter, softened
2-1/2 c. mixed shredded cheese
   blend (such as Swiss, Italian
   or casserole style)
1/2 to 3/4 c. milk, warmed
4 slices bacon, crisply cooked
   and crumbled
2 t. dried sage
salt and pepper to taste
Optional: additional
   shredded cheese

73

Cover potatoes with water in a
large saucepan. Bring to a boil;
cook until tender, 15 to 18 minutes.
Drain potatoes; place in a large bowl
and mash. Blend in butter and
cheese; add milk to make a creamy
consistency. Stir in bacon and sage;
add salt and pepper to taste. Sprinkle
with additional cheese, if desired.
Makes 8 servings.

Carolen Collins
Kansas City, MO

These cheesy mashed
potatoes are out of
this world!

4-Cheese Mac & Cheese

1/4 c. all-purpose flour
1/8 t. pepper
2-1/2 c. milk
1/2 c. grated Parmesan cheese
1/2 c. shredded sharp Cheddar
   cheese
3/4 c. pasteurized process cheese
   spread, cubed
1/4 c. cream cheese, cubed
8-oz. pkg. rotini pasta, cooked
1/3 c. onion-flavored Melba toast,
   crushed
1 T. butter, melted

Combine flour and pepper in a
saucepan; whisk in milk until smooth.
Bring to a boil over medium heat;
cook for one minute, stirring
constantly. Reduce heat; add cheeses,
stirring until melted. Remove from
heat; stir in pasta and pour into a
greased 9"x9" baking pan. Combine
toast crumbs and butter; sprinkle on
top. Bake, uncovered, at 350 degrees
for 30 minutes, or until bubbly and
golden. Serves 6.

Tami Bowman
Gooseberry Patch
We like rotini because
the spirals really grab
the sauce...yum!

Campers' Beans

6 to 8 slices bacon
1 onion, chopped
1/4 c. brown sugar, packed
1/4 c. catsup
2 T. mustard
2 t. vinegar
2 32-oz. cans baked beans

Crisply cook bacon in a skillet over medium-high heat. When partially cooked, add onion. Continue cooking until bacon is crisp. Drain bacon and onion on a paper towel; crumble bacon. Combine brown sugar, catsup, mustard and vinegar in a large saucepan; simmer over low heat for 15 minutes. Stir in beans, bacon and onion. Simmer, uncovered, for at least 30 minutes, stirring occasionally. If desired, garnish with additional bacon. Makes 8 to 10 servings.

75

Janie Collins
Freeport, PA
Sweet and satisfying...
almost a meal in itself!

Country Potato Bake

20-oz. pkg. frozen shredded
   hashbrowns
10-3/4 oz. can cream of
   chicken soup
1 c. sour cream
1/4 c. margarine, melted
1 c. shredded Cheddar cheese
6 slices bacon, crisply cooked
   and chopped
2.8-oz. can French fried onions

Spread hashbrowns evenly in the
bottom of a greased 13"x9" baking pan.
Mix soup, sour cream and margarine
together; spread over hashbrowns.
Sprinkle with cheese, bacon and
onions. Bake, covered, at 350 degrees
for 45 minutes. Makes 10 servings.

Penny Frazier
Kokomo, IN

Using frozen hashbrowns,
this scrumptious side is
oven-ready in a jiffy.

Famous Broccoli Casserole

16-oz. pkg. frozen broccoli
10-oz. pkg. frozen broccoli
2 10-3/4 oz. cans cream of
  chicken soup
16-oz. pkg. pasteurized process
  cheese spread, cubed
2 6.9-oz. pkgs. chicken-flavored
  rice vermicelli mix, prepared

Cook and drain broccoli; place
in a slow cooker. Add soup and
cheese; mix well. Stir in prepared
rice vermicelli mix. Cover and
cook on low setting for 3 to 4 hours,
until hot and bubbly. Makes
32 servings.

77

Paul Gaulke
Gooseberry Patch

This casserole recipe is
tried & true...we can't
imagine a Gooseberry Patch
potluck without it!

Crunchy Apple-Pear Salad

2 apples, cored and cubed
2 pears, cored and thinly sliced
1 T. lemon juice
2 heads butter lettuce, torn into
   bite-size pieces
1/2 c. crumbled gorgonzola
   cheese
1 c. oil
6 T. cider vinegar
1/2 c. sugar
1 t. celery seed
1/2 t. salt
1/4 t. pepper
1/2 c. chopped walnuts, toasted

Toss apples and pears with lemon juice; drain. Arrange lettuce on 6 salad plates; top with apples, pears and cheese. Combine remaining ingredients except walnuts in a jar with a tight-fitting lid. Cover; shake well until dressing is blended and sugar dissolves. Drizzle salad with dressing; sprinkle with walnuts. Serve immediately. Serves 6.

Sharon Wilson
Palmyra, PA

Toss together green Granny Smith apples with red Anjou or Bartlett pears...so colorful!

Dilly Casserole Bread

1 env. active dry yeast
1/4 c. warm water
1 c. cottage cheese
2 T. sugar
1 T. dried minced onion
2 T. butter, softened and divided
2 t. dill weed, divided
1-1/2 t. salt, divided
1/4 t. baking soda
1 egg, beaten
2-1/4 to 2-1/2 c. all-purpose
   flour

Soften yeast in very warm water, about 110 to 115 degrees. Combine cottage cheese, sugar, onion, one tablespoon butter, one teaspoon dill weed, one teaspoon salt, baking soda, egg and yeast mixture in a medium bowl. Add flour to make a stiff dough. Cover and let rise until double in size, about 40 minutes. Stir dough down; place in a greased 9"x5" loaf pan. Let rise again for 40 minutes. Bake at 350 degrees for 35 to 40 minutes, or until golden. Brush with remaining butter; sprinkle with remaining dill weed and salt. Makes one loaf.

Margie Schaffner
Altoona, IA

This recipe has been in our family for years...there's nothing better than warm, fresh-baked bread!

Granny's Country Cornbread

1-1/4 c. cornmeal
3/4 c. all-purpose flour
5 T. sugar
2 t. baking powder
1/2 t. salt
1 c. buttermilk
1/3 c. oil
1 egg, beaten
1 c. shredded sharp Cheddar
    cheese
1 c. corn
1 T. jalapeño pepper, minced

Mix together cornmeal, flour, sugar, baking powder and salt in a large bowl. Make a well in center; pour in buttermilk, oil and egg. Stir just until ingredients are lightly moistened. Fold in cheese, corn and jalapeño; pour into a greased 8" cast-iron skillet. Bake at 375 degrees for 20 minutes, or until a tester inserted in the center comes out clean. Let cool slightly; cut into wedges. Makes 4 to 6 servings.

Rachel Anderson
Livermore, CA

Pour the batter into vintage corn stick pans... the kids will love 'em!

Chicken Taco Salad

8 6-inch flour tortillas
2 c. cooked chicken breast,
  shredded
1-1/4 oz. pkg. taco seasoning mix
3/4 c. water
2 c. shredded lettuce
15-1/2 oz. can black beans,
  drained and rinsed
1-1/2 c. shredded Cheddar cheese
2 tomatoes, chopped
1/2 c. green onion, sliced
15-1/4 oz. can corn, drained
2-1/4 oz. can sliced black
  olives, drained
1 avocado, pitted, peeled
  and cubed
Garnish: sour cream, salsa

Microwave tortillas on high setting
for one minute, or until softened.
Press each tortilla into an ungreased
muffin cup to form a bowl shape.
Bake at 350 degrees for 10 minutes;
cool. Combine chicken, taco seasoning
and water in a skillet over medium
heat. Cook, stirring frequently, until
blended, about 5 minutes. Divide
lettuce among tortilla bowls. Top
with chicken and other ingredients,
garnishing with a dollop of sour cream
and salsa. Makes 8 servings.

Abby Snay
San Francisco, CA
Crisp tortilla cups
jam-packed with yummy
ingredients!

81

Chocolate Bread Pudding

2 c. milk
6 slices white bread, crusts
    trimmed
1/2 c. sugar
1/3 c. baking cocoa
2 eggs, separated and divided
2 T. butter, melted
1 t. vanilla extract
1/2 c. semi-sweet chocolate chunks
Garnish: whipped cream,
    baking cocoa

Heat milk in a large saucepan just until tiny bubbles form; remove from heat. Cube bread and add to milk; stir until smooth. Add sugar, cocoa and egg yolks; stir until well blended. Add butter and vanilla; set aside. Beat egg whites until stiff peaks form; fold into mixture along with chocolate chunks. Pour into 6 lightly greased custard cups; set cups in a larger pan filled with one inch of hot water. Bake at 350 degrees for 40 minutes, or until firm. Garnish with whipped cream and baking cocoa; serve warm or cold. Makes 6 servings.

Gail Bamford
Vienna, VA

Just like Grandma's,
with a twist of cocoa to
tempt your sweet tooth.

Cinnamon-Apple Parfaits

1 c. quick-cooking oats,
  uncooked
1/2 c. brown sugar, packed
1/4 c. butter, melted
21 oz. can apple pie filling,
  warmed
1/4 t. cinnamon
1 qt. vanilla ice cream, slightly
  softened

Combine oats, brown sugar and
butter; spread in an ungreased
8"x8" baking pan. Bake at
350 degrees for 10 minutes.
Cool; crumble and set aside.
Mix together pie filling and
cinnamon; divide among 8 parfait
glasses. Top with softened ice cream
and crumbled oat mixture. Serves 8.

83

Courtney Robinson
Delaware, OH
A yummy, warm parfait. The
baked oat crumble is
delicious...try it as an
ice cream topping too.

Summertime Strawberry Shortcake

3 to 4 c. strawberries, hulled
  and sliced
1/2 c. plus 2 T. sugar, divided
2 c. all-purpose flour
1 T. baking powder
1/2 t. salt
3/4 c. butter, divided
1 egg, beaten
2/3 c. light cream
1 c. whipping cream, whipped

Toss strawberries with 1/2 cup sugar and set aside. Combine flour, remaining sugar, baking powder and salt in a separate bowl. Cut in 1/2 cup butter until mixture forms coarse crumbs; set aside. Whisk together egg and light cream; add to flour mixture, stirring just until moistened. Divide dough into 6 parts; pat into biscuits and place on a greased baking sheet. Bake at 450 degrees for 8 to 10 minutes, until golden. Cool biscuits briefly on a wire rack. Split in half with a serrated knife; spread bottoms with remaining butter. Top with berries and whipped cream; add tops. Garnish with remaining berries and cream. Makes 6 servings.

Martha Doyle
Rome, NY

Quick & easy...make one big shortcake! Pat dough into a greased 8" round cake pan and bake for 15 to 18 minutes.

Very Berry Peach Pies

4 c. peaches, pitted, peeled
   and sliced
1-1/2 c. blackberries
1 c. blueberries
3/4 c. sugar
1/4 c. all-purpose flour
2 T. butter, diced
2 9-inch pie crusts
Garnish: cinnamon-sugar

Combine fruit in a large bowl;
mix gently. Blend 3/4 cup sugar
and flour in a small bowl; toss
lightly with fruit mixture. Pour
fruit mixture into six to eight,
8" individual ramekins; dot with
butter. Gently roll out dough on a
floured surface and cut six to eight
circles one inch larger than ramekins.
Place crusts atop ramekins. Trim and
crimp edges; cut vents in crust.
Sprinkle with cinnamon-sugar. Cover
edges of crust with strips of aluminum
foil to prevent overbrowning. Bake at
425 degrees for 40 to 45 minutes,
until golden. Makes 6 to 8 servings.

Wanda Niles
Costa Mesa, CA
I like to vent the crusts
in these little pies with
a mini cookie cutter.

Chewy Chocolate Chip Cookies

Michelle Sheridan
Gooseberry Patch

Everyone's all-time favorite cookie...they travel well too!

1/2 c. butter, softened
1/2 c. brown sugar, packed
1/2 c. sugar
1 egg, beaten
1/2 t. vanilla extract
1 c. plus 2 T. all-purpose flour
1/2 t. salt
1/2 t. baking soda
1/2 c. chopped nuts
1/2 c. semi-sweet chocolate chips

Blend together butter and sugars until creamy. Beat in egg and vanilla; set aside. Combine flour, salt and baking soda; mix well and stir into butter mixture. Fold in nuts and chocolate chips. Drop by teaspoonfuls, 2 inches apart, on greased baking sheets. Bake at 375 degrees for 10 minutes, or until golden. Makes 2 dozen.

Hokey-Pokey Cupcakes

18-1/4 oz. pkg. white cake mix
3-oz. pkg. orange gelatin mix
1 c. boiling water
16-oz. container favorite-flavor
   frosting

Prepare cake mix according to
package directions, using egg white
version. Spoon into 24 paper-lined
muffin cups; bake as directed. Let
cool in pan for 15 minutes. Spray a
large fork with non stick vegetable
spray; pierce cupcakes with fork at
1/4-inch intervals. Place cupcakes
on a paper towel-lined tray; set aside.
Add gelatin mix to boiling water,
stirring until dissolved; spoon over
cupcakes. Chill cupcakes for 3 hours.
Frost and garnish as desired. Makes
2 dozen.

Veva Banks
Neosho, MO

These scrumptious cupcakes
have a surprise swirl of
fruit flavor inside.

Streusel-Topped Raspberry Bars

2-1/4 c. all-purpose flour
1 c. sugar
1 c. chopped pecans
1 c. butter, softened
1 egg
1 c. raspberry preserves
Garnish: powdered sugar

Combine flour, sugar, pecans, butter
and egg in a large bowl. Beat with an
electric mixer on low speed for 2 to
3 minutes. Set aside 2 cups of mixture
for topping. Press remaining mixture
into bottom of a greased 13"x9" baking
pan. Spread preserves over top;
sprinkle with reserved pecan mixture.
Bake at 350 degrees for 40 to
50 minutes, until lightly golden.
Cool completely; cut into bars and
sprinkle with powdered sugar.
Makes 2 dozen.

Sue Fine
San Diego, CA
Just the thing
for a mid-morning
coffee break!

Rocky Road Bars

22-1/2 oz. pkg. brownie mix with
   chocolate syrup pouch
1/4 c. water
1/3 c. oil
2 eggs, beaten
12-oz. pkg. semi-sweet chocolate
   chips, divided
1-1/2 to 2 c. mini marshmallows
1-1/2 c. dry-roasted peanuts,
   chopped

Grease bottom only of a
13"x9" baking pan; set aside.
Combine brownie mix, syrup
pouch, water, oil and eggs; stir
until well blended. Mix in one cup
chocolate chips; spread in baking
pan. Bake at 350 degrees for 30 to
35 minutes, or until a toothpick
inserted 2 inches from side of pan
comes out clean. Immediately
sprinkle with marshmallows,
remaining chocolate chips and
peanuts. Cover pan with a baking
sheet for 2 to 3 minutes; remove
and cool completely. Cut into bars;
store tightly covered. Makes 2 dozen.

89

Dale-Harriet Rogovich
Madison, WI

Brownies with chocolate
chips, marshmallows and
peanuts...need I say more?

Frosted Sugar Cookies

2 c. butter, softened
1-1/3 c. sugar
2 eggs, beaten
2 t. vanilla extract
5 c. all-purpose flour
Garnish: colored sugar

Blend butter and sugar together; stir in eggs and vanilla. Add flour; mix until well blended. Shape into a ball; cover and chill for 4 hours to overnight. Roll out dough 1/4-inch thick on a lightly floured surface; cut out with cookie cutters as desired. Arrange cookies on lightly greased baking sheets. Bake at 350 degrees for 8 to 10 minutes, until golden. Frost cookies when cool; decorate as desired. Makes 4 dozen.

Frosting:

4-1/2 c. powdered sugar
6 T. butter, melted
6 T. milk
2 T. vanilla extract
1 T. lemon juice
Optional: food coloring

Combine all ingredients in a medium bowl. Beat with an electric mixer on low speed until smooth.

June Lemen
Nashua, NH
We love to bake cut-out cookies year 'round for holidays...you can't beat this recipe!

Grandma Gracie's Lemon Cake

18-1/4 oz. pkg. yellow cake mix
3.4-oz. pkg. instant lemon
   pudding mix
3/4 c. oil
3/4 c. water
4 eggs, beaten
Garnish: powdered sugar

Combine all ingredients; mix well.
Pour into a greased 13"x9" baking
pan. Bake at 350 degrees for
35 to 40 minutes, or until a
toothpick inserted in center comes
out clean. Immediately poke holes
through cake with a fork; pour glaze
over cake. Dust with powdered sugar.
Serves 10 to 12.

Glaze:

2 c. powdered sugar
2 T. butter, melted
2 T. water
1/3 c. lemon juice

Combine all ingredients; stir
until smooth.

Denise Musgrave
Shelbyville, IN
One of my grandmother's
best recipes. She was an
excellent cook for her
6 kids, 18 grandkids and
35 great-grandkids.

Peanut Butter Bars

1-1/2 c. graham cracker crumbs
1 c. margarine, melted
16-oz. pkg. powdered sugar
1 c. creamy peanut butter
12-oz. pkg. butterscotch chips

Combine graham cracker crumbs, margarine, powdered sugar and peanut butter; mix well. Press into the bottom of a lightly greased 13"x9" baking pan; set aside. Melt butterscotch chips in a double boiler; spread over crumb mixture. Refrigerate for several hours to overnight, until firm. Cut into bars. Makes 2 dozen.

Angela Sims
Willow Springs, IL
Make a good thing even better...drizzle with melted chocolate. Yum!

Chocolate Tartlets

2 9-inch pie crusts
2/3 c. whipping cream
3 1-oz. sqs. semi-sweet baking
   chocolate, chopped
3 1-oz. sqs. sweet baking
   chocolate, chopped
Garnish: whipped cream,
   raspberries

On a floured surface, roll out
pie crusts to 1/8-inch thick. Cut
out 24 circles with a 2-3/4 inch
round biscuit cutter. Fit carefully
into mini muffin cups, pressing
edges against rims and crimping
with a fork. Bake at 350 degrees
for 7 to 10 minutes, until set and
golden. Cool. In a heavy saucepan,
bring cream just to simmering over
medium heat. Remove from heat; add
chocolates and let stand 2 minutes.
Whisk until melted; transfer to a
medium bowl. Cover and chill for
one hour. Beat chocolate mixture
with an electric mixer on medium
speed until soft peaks form. Spoon
into baked crusts; chill. At serving
time, garnish with dollops of
whipped cream and raspberries.
Makes 2 dozen.

93

Emily Plotnick
West Linn, OR
Delectable on a
dessert buffet.

Crustless Pumpkin Pie

4 eggs, beaten
15-oz. can pumpkin
12-oz. can evaporated milk
1-1/2 c. sugar
2 t. pumpkin pie spice
1 t. salt
18-1/2 oz. pkg. yellow cake mix
1 c. chopped pecans or walnuts
1 c. butter, melted
Optional: whipped topping,
    chopped nuts, cinnamon

Combine eggs, pumpkin, evaporated milk, sugar, spice and salt. Mix well; pour into an ungreased 13"x9" baking pan. Sprinkle dry cake mix and nuts over top. Drizzle with butter; do not stir. Bake at 350 degrees for 45 minutes to one hour, testing for doneness with a toothpick. Serve with whipped topping, sprinkled with nuts and cinnamon. Makes 8 to 10 servings.

Linda Webb
Delaware, OH
My favorite pumpkin dessert...too good to save only for Thanksgiving!

Autumn Apple Pie

1/2 c. plus 1 T. sugar, divided
6 Granny Smith apples, cored,
  peeled and thinly sliced
3 T. lemon juice
1/2 c. brown sugar, packed
2 t. cinnamon
1/4 t. nutmeg
3 T. all-purpose flour
1/4 c. butter, chilled and diced
9 caramels, unwrapped and
  quartered
2 9-inch pie crusts

95

Combine 1/2 cup sugar and all
remaining ingredients except crusts.
Stir until mixture evenly coats apples.
Line a 9" pie plate with one pie crust;
spoon filling into crust. Cover with
second crust; flute edges and vent
as desired. Sprinkle remaining sugar
over crust. Place on an aluminum
foil-covered baking sheet. Bake at
375 degrees for 30 minutes. Reduce
heat to 350 degrees; bake an additional
20 minutes, until crust is golden.
Serves 6 to 8.

Cheryl Musial
Acworth, GA
Cortland and Pippin apples
are wonderful in
this pie too.

Raspberry Truffle Cheesecake

18 chocolate sandwich cookies,
  crushed
2 T. butter, melted
4 8-oz. pkgs. cream cheese,
  softened and divided
1-1/4 c. sugar
3 eggs
1 c. sour cream
1 t. almond extract
2 6-oz. pkgs. semi-sweet chocolate
  chips, divided
1/3 c. raspberry preserves
1/4 c. whipping cream

Combine cookie crumbs and butter; press into bottom of a 9" springform pan. Combine 3 packages cream cheese and sugar; beat with an electric mixer on medium speed until blended. Add eggs, one at a time, mixing well after each. Blend in sour cream and extract; pour over crust. Melt one package chocolate chips over low heat. Combine with remaining cream cheese and preserves; mix well and drop by rounded tablespoonfuls over plain cream cheese mixture. Bake at 325 degrees for one hour and 20 minutes. Cool; remove sides of pan. Melt remaining chocolate chips with cream over low heat, stirring until smooth. Spread over cheesecake, drizzling over sides. Chill for 4 hours. Makes 12 to 14 servings.

Deborah Hilton
Oswego, NY

Garnish with plump raspberries and sprigs of fresh mint...fabulous!

Mandarin Orange Cake

18-1/2 oz. pkg. white cake mix
11-oz. can mandarin oranges,
    drained and juice reserved
3 egg whites
1/2 c. oil
2 8-oz. cans crushed pineapple
3-1/2 oz. pkg. instant vanilla
    pudding mix
8-oz. container frozen whipped
    topping, thawed
1 c. sweetened flaked coconut,
    divided

97

Combine cake mix, reserved juice,
egg whites and oil. Blend with an
electric mixer on medium speed
for 2 minutes, until creamy. Fold
in oranges; pour into a greased and
floured 13"x9" baking pan. Bake at
350 degrees for 25 to 35 minutes,
until a toothpick in the center comes
out clean. Place pan on a wire rack
to cool completely. Pour pineapple
and its juice into a medium bowl;
stir in pudding mix. Fold in whipped
topping and 1/2 cup coconut. Mix
well; chill while cake is cooling.
Spread over top and sides; sprinkle
with remaining coconut. Serve
immediately or keep refrigerated.
Serves 12.

Nancy Likens
Wooster, OH

My daughter's favorite
cake...the one she always
requests for her birthday!

Rustic Peach Tart

9-inch pie crust
3/4 c. plus 2 T. sugar, divided
1/3 c. all-purpose flour
1/2 t. ground ginger
1/4 t. nutmeg
16-oz. pkg. frozen sliced peaches

On a floured surface, roll out pie crust into a 12-inch circle. Place on an ungreased baking sheet and set aside. Mix 3/4 cup sugar, flour and spices; add frozen peach slices and toss to coat. Spoon peaches onto crust to within 2 inches of edge. Gently fold over edge of crust to form a 2-inch border, pleating as you go. Moisten crust edge with water; sprinkle with remaining sugar. Bake at 425 degrees until golden, about 15 minutes; reduce temperature to 350 degrees and bake until bubbly, about 30 to 35 minutes more. Makes 8 servings.

Jeni Steenblock
Des Moines, IA

Oh-so easy to make...
you'll want to try
other fruit too!

Apple-Cranberry Crisp

6 c. Golden Delicious or
   Winesap apples, cored,
   peeled and sliced
3 c. cranberries
1 c. sugar
2 t. cinnamon
1 to 2 t. lemon juice
3/4 c. butter, sliced and divided
1 c. all-purpose flour
1 c. brown sugar, packed
Garnish: vanilla ice cream

99

Toss together apple slices,
cranberries, sugar and cinnamon.
Spread in a greased 13"x9" baking
pan. Sprinkle with lemon juice; dot
with 1/4 cup butter. Blend remaining
butter with flour and brown sugar
until crumbly; sprinkle over apple
mixture. Bake at 350 degrees for
one hour. Serve warm with ice cream.
Serves 10 to 12.

Brenda Derby
Northborough, MA

A must-have at
our holiday dinners.

Carrot Cake

2 c. all-purpose flour
2 t. baking powder
1-1/2 t. baking soda
1 t. salt
2 t. cinnamon
3/4 c. oil
2 c. sugar
4 eggs, beaten
2 c. carrots, peeled and grated
15-1/4 oz. can crushed pineapple

Combine all ingredients; blend well
and pour into a greased and floured
Bundt® pan. Bake at 325 degrees for
40 to 45 minutes, or until cake tests
done with a toothpick. Cool; frost
while still warm. Makes 12 to
15 servings.

Frosting:

1/2 c. margarine, softened
8-oz. pkg. cream cheese, softened
1 t. vanilla extract
16-oz. pkg. powdered sugar

Blend ingredients together until
smooth and creamy.

Sheri Fitzsimmons
Caledonia, MI

Moist and delicious...
just what carrot cake
should be.

Caramel Rolls

1 c. brown sugar, packed
1 c. whipping cream
3-1/2 c. all-purpose flour, divided
3/4 c. sugar, divided
1 t. salt
1 env. active dry yeast
1 c. water
1/2 c. plus 2 T. butter, divided
1 egg, beaten
2 t. cinnamon

Combine brown sugar and cream in an ungreased 13"x9" baking pan; set aside. In a large bowl, blend 1-1/2 cups flour, 1/4 cup sugar, salt and yeast. Heat water and 2 tablespoons butter until very warm; add warm liquid and egg to flour mixture. With an electric mixer on low speed, beat until moistened; beat at medium speed for 3 minutes. Stir in remaining flour. Knead for 2 to 3 minutes on a floured surface; roll out to a 15-inch by 7-inch rectangle. Combine remaining sugar, remaining butter and cinnamon; spread over dough. Starting at long side, roll up tightly, sealing edges. Slice into 15 rolls. Place rolls, cut-side down, in prepared pan. Cover and let rise in a warm place until double in size, 35 to 45 minutes. Bake at 400 degrees for 20 to 25 minutes, until golden. Makes 15 rolls.

Lisa Colombo
Appleton, WI
Only the freshest butter will do for Grandma's homemade caramel rolls!

Praline Pecan Mini Cakes

Nichole Martelli
Santa Fe, TX
A scrumptious recipe...
too good not to share!

18-1/4 oz. pkg. butter pecan cake mix
16-oz. container coconut-pecan
  frosting
4 eggs, beaten
3/4 c. oil
1 c. water
1 c. chopped pecans, divided

Combine all ingredients except pecans; mix well. Stir in half the pecans. Divide remaining pecans among twelve, lightly greased mini Bundt® pans; pour batter over pecans to fill 2/3 full. Bake at 350 degrees for 50 minutes, or until a toothpick inserted near the center comes out clean. Cool slightly; turn out cakes and drizzle with frosting. Makes one dozen.

Caramel Frosting:

1/4 c. butter
1/2 c. brown sugar, packed
2 c. powdered sugar
1/8 to 1/4 c. heavy whipping cream

Melt butter in a saucepan over medium heat. Add brown sugar; cook and stir to boiling. Cook for one minute, until slightly thickened. Cool; stir in powdered sugar and 1/8 cup cream. Add remaining cream to make a drizzling consistency.

Easy Cherry Cobbler

15-oz. can tart red cherries
1 c. all-purpose flour
1-1/4 c. sugar, divided
1 c. milk
2 t. baking powder
1/8 t. salt
1/2 c. butter, melted
Optional: vanilla ice cream or
    whipped cream

In a saucepan over medium heat, cook cherries with their juice until boiling; remove from heat. In a medium bowl, mix flour, one cup sugar, milk, baking powder and salt. Spread butter in a 2-quart casserole dish or in 4 to 6 one-cup ramekins; pour flour mixture over butter. Add cherries; do not stir. Sprinkle remaining sugar over top. Bake at 400 degrees for 20 to 30 minutes. Serve warm, garnished as desired. Makes 4 to 6 servings.

103

Melonie Klosterhoff
Fairbanks, AK

If they're available,
use fresh-from-the-farm
cherries for a
special treat!

Mom's Monster Cookies

6 eggs, beaten
1 c. margarine
16-oz. pkg. brown sugar
2 c. sugar
2 T. vanilla extract
6 T. corn syrup
3 c. creamy peanut butter
4 t. baking soda
9 c. quick-cooking oats, uncooked
1-1/2 c. semi-sweet chocolate chips
1-1/2 c. peanuts
1-1/2 c. candy-coated chocolates

In a large bowl, mix ingredients in order listed. Drop by rounded teaspoonfuls onto ungreased baking sheets. Bake at 350 degrees for 12 to 16 minutes, until golden. Makes 10 to 12 dozen.

Susie Backus
Gooseberry Patch

Packed with goodies...
chocolate chips, candies,
peanuts, chewy oats
and more!

Texas Sheet Cake

1 c. margarine
1 c. water
6 T. baking cocoa
2 c. all-purpose flour
2 c. sugar
1/2 t. cinnamon
1/2 t. salt
2 eggs, beaten
8-oz. container sour cream
1 t. baking soda
Garnish: chopped walnuts

Combine margarine, water and cocoa in a saucepan over medium heat. Bring to a boil; remove from heat. Mix flour, sugar, cinnamon and salt; stir into hot mixture. Mix remaining ingredients except nuts; add to batter and mix well. Pour into a greased 15"x10" jelly-roll pan. Bake at 350 degrees for 22 minutes. Pour icing over cake while hot; sprinkle with nuts. Makes 20 servings.

Icing:

1/2 c. margarine
4 T. baking cocoa
6 T. milk
16-oz. pkg. powdered sugar
1 t. vanilla extract

Bring margarine, cocoa and milk to a boil; remove from heat. Stir in powdered sugar and vanilla.

Doris Stegner
Gooseberry Patch

Round up your family & friends for this wonderful Texas-size cake.

Eclair Cake

1 c. water
1/2 c. butter
1 c. all-purpose flour
4 eggs, beaten
8-oz. pkg. cream cheese, softened
3 c. milk
2 3-oz. pkgs. instant vanilla
    pudding mix
8-oz. container frozen whipped
    topping, thawed
Garnish: chocolate syrup

Combine water and butter in a saucepan; heat until boiling. Whisk in flour until smooth; remove from heat. Pour mixture into a medium bowl; gradually blend in eggs. Spread in a greased 13"x9" baking pan; bake at 350 degrees for 30 minutes. Remove from oven; press baked crust down lightly and set aside. With an electric mixer on medium speed, beat together cream cheese, milk and pudding mix for 2 minutes; spread over crust. Refrigerate until firm. At serving time, spread with whipped topping; drizzle with chocolate syrup. Serves 12 to 15.

Cheryl Frost
Woodstock, OH

Luscious cream filling
and chocolatey topping...
best with a tall,
cold glass of milk!

Fudge Brownie Pie

1 c. sugar
1/2 c. margarine, melted
2 eggs, beaten
1/2 c. all-purpose flour
1/3 c. baking cocoa
1/4 t. salt
1 t. vanilla extract
1/2 c. chopped walnuts
Garnish: vanilla ice cream

Beat sugar and margarine together.
Add eggs; mix well. Stir in flour,
cocoa and salt; mix in vanilla and
nuts. Pour into a greased and
floured 9" pie plate; bake at
350 degrees for 25 to 30 minutes.
Cut into wedges; top with scoops of
ice cream. Serves 6 to 8.

107

Flo Burtnett
Gage, OK

Just as good now as
back in 1914, when it
first appeared in
a YMCA cookbook.

INDEX

INDEX

Our Story

Back in 1984, we were next-door neighbors raising our families in the little town of Delaware, Ohio. Two moms with small children, we were looking for a way to do what we loved and stay home with the kids too. We had always shared a love of home cooking and making memories with family & friends and so, after many a conversation over the backyard fence, **Gooseberry Patch** was born.

We put together our first catalog at our kitchen tables, enlisting the help of our loved ones wherever we could. From that very first mailing, we found an immediate connection with many of our customers and it wasn't long before we began receiving letters, photos and recipes from these new friends. In 1992, we put together our very first cookbook, compiled from hundreds of these recipes and, the rest, as they say, is history.

Hard to believe it's been over 25 years since those kitchen-table days! From that original little **Gooseberry Patch** family, we've grown to include an amazing group of creative folks who love cooking, decorating and creating as much as we do. Today, we're best known for our homestyle, family-friendly cookbooks, now recognized as national bestsellers.

JoAnn & Vickie

One thing's for sure, we couldn't have done it without our friends all across the country. Each year, we're honored to turn thousands of your recipes into our collectible cookbooks. Our hope is that each book captures the stories and heart of all of you who have shared with us. Whether you've been with us since the beginning or are just discovering us, welcome to the **Gooseberry Patch** family!

Visit us online:
www.gooseberrypatch.com
1•800•854•6673

U.S. to Canadian Recipe Equivalents

Volume Measurements

1/4 teaspoon	1 mL
1/2 teaspoon	2 mL
1 teaspoon	5 mL
1 tablespoon = 3 teaspoons	15 mL
2 tablespoons = 1 fluid ounce	30 mL
1/4 cup	60 mL
1/3 cup	75 mL
1/2 cup = 4 fluid ounces	125 mL
1 cup = 8 fluid ounces	250 mL
2 cups = 1 pint =16 fluid ounces	500 mL
4 cups = 1 quart	1 L

Weights

1 ounce	30 g
4 ounces	120 g
8 ounces	225 g
16 ounces = 1 pound	450 g

Oven Temperatures

300° F	150° C
325° F	160° C
350° F	180° C
375° F	190° C
400° F	200° C
450° F	230° C

Baking Pan Sizes

Square

8x8x2 inches	2 L = 20x20x5 cm
9x9x2 inches	2.5 L = 23x23x5 cm

Rectangular

13x9x2 inches	3.5 L = 33x23x5 cm

Loaf

9x5x3 inches	2 L = 23x13x7 cm

Round

8x1-1/2 inches	1.2 L = 20x4 cm
9x1-1/2 inches	1.5 L = 23x4 cm

Recipe Abbreviations

t. = teaspoon	ltr. = liter
T. = tablespoon	oz. = ounce
c. = cup	lb. = pound
pt. = pint	doz. = dozen
qt. = quart	pkg. = package
gal. = gallon	env. = envelope

Kitchen Measurements

A pinch = 1/8 tablespoon
3 teaspoons = 1 tablespoon
2 tablespoons = 1/8 cup
4 tablespoons = 1/4 cup
8 tablespoons = 1/2 cup
16 tablespoons = 1 cup
2 cups = 1 pint
4 cups = 1 quart
4 quarts = 1 gallon

1 fluid ounce = 2 tablespoons
4 fluid ounces = 1/2 cup
8 fluid ounces = 1 cup
16 fluid ounces = 1 pint
32 fluid ounces = 1 quart
16 ounces net weight = 1 pound